Jesus' 30 recorded healings are retold in the following books:

Jesus' Healings, Part 1

Man Healed of Mental Illness (Capernaum)
Peter's Mother-in-Law Healed of Fever
Man Healed of Leprosy
Man Healed of Paralysis
Man with Withered Hand Healed
Nobleman's Son Healed of Illness
Centurion's Servant Healed of Paralysis
Widow's Son Brought Back to Life
Woman Healed of Sin
Man Healed of Blindness and Dumbness

Jesus' Healings, Part 2

Man Healed of Mental Illness (Gadara)
Jairus' Daughter Brought Back to Life
Woman Healed of Illness
Two Men Healed of Blindness
Man Healed of Dumbness
Man Healed of Disability
Woman's Daughter Healed of Illness
Man Healed of Deafness and Speech Problems
Man Healed of Blindness
Man's Son Healed of Epilepsy

Jesus' Healings, Part 3

Woman Healed of Back Problem
Man Healed of Swelling
Ten Men Healed of Leprosy
Woman Healed of Adultery
Man Healed of Blindness from Birth
Lazarus Brought Back to Life
Bartimaeus Healed of Blindness
Zacchaeus Healed of Dishonesty
Malchus' Ear Healed
Jesus' Resurrection

Jesus' healings
Part 1

Written by

Mary Jo Beebe
Olene E. Carroll
Nancy H. Fischer

Illustrated by

Genevieve Meek

Table of Contents

GENERAL PUBLICATIONS
BIBLE PRODUCTS, CSPS
Boston, Massachusetts, U.S.A.

ISBN: : 0-87510-400-2
© 2002 General Publications Bible Products, CSPS
Printed in the United States of America

Introduction

About the Book

Jesus' Healings, Part 1, is the first in a three-part series. The three books are written for all ages—children, teenagers, and adults—anyone who is interested in the great healing work of Jesus.

All 30 of Jesus' Healings Included

The three books bring to life in simple language the 30 recorded healings of Christ Jesus. These healings span a period of possibly three years in Jesus' life. They include healings of sickness and sin, as well as four accounts of restoring life, one of them being Jesus' own resurrection.

Stories Arranged in Chronological Order

We have attempted to place the healings in chronological order according to Bible scholars. Not one of the Gospel writers includes all 30 of the healings. Some of the stories are found in only one Gospel book. In some cases, stories can be found in two of the books, sometimes in three, and two of them in all four. As a result, no exact chronology is known.

Account Chosen Based on Detail

When more than one account of a healing story occurs, in most cases we have chosen the account that is the richest in detail. When there are significant details in another account, we have added that information in sidebars.

Stories—Self-Contained

Each of the healing stories in the book is self-contained, with references to other pages in the book for definitions and commentary. While this feature is helpful for reading and studying individual stories, we recommend that you take the time to read the book from beginning to end as well. This will give you a full and inspired understanding of the scope and importance of Jesus' healings.

Written in Simple Language

The stories are written in contemporary English and at a level young children can understand. Sidebars provide additional information and commentary about the stories that will be interesting to older children and adults. In a few of the stories, passages too difficult for young children to understand have been placed in sidebars.

While every attempt has been made to write the stories in simple language, some stories may still be beyond the understanding of very young children. Parents and teachers must use their own discretion about the appropriateness of stories. In some cases, it may be helpful to paraphrase a story or leave out certain sections.

Details and Ideas Added for Understanding

In writing the stories, we have added details and ideas with the intent of making the stories more understandable. The details are supported by authoritative Bible scholars. You can find sources in the bibliography on page 59.

Based on Concepts in the Bible and *Science and Health with Key to the Scriptures*

In the healing stories, we have identified spiritual truths that were the foundation of Jesus' healings. These truths are based on concepts found in the Bible and in *Science and Health with Key to the Scriptures* by Mary Baker Eddy. *Science and Health* provides inspiring insights into the Scriptures, helping the reader recognize the spiritual ideas that were so important in Jesus' healings. These include Jesus' spiritual understanding of God, which enabled him to see beyond the material senses and to affirm the spiritual reality.

Introduction

Special Features of the Book

Jesus' Healings includes features you may want to explore before you read the stories. Understanding how the book is organized and arranged will enhance your enjoyment of it.

Sidebars like this provide information about a bolded word or phrase in the story.

Sidebars like this show where information can be found in another story about a bolded word or phrase in the story.

Sidebars like this provide commentary or information from another Gospel account. The sidebar color matches a colored square in the story for easy reference.

NOTE: All Bible quotations in sidebars are from the King James Version.

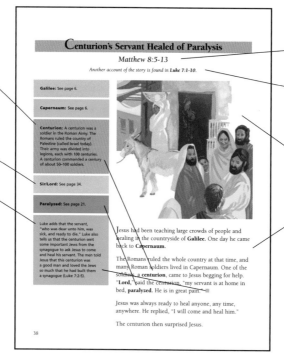

Bible book and verses where the story can be found.

Bible books and verses where other accounts of the story can be found.

Illustrations enhance children's (and adults') understanding and enjoyment of the stories.

The text is easily read and understood by all ages.

The end of each story is indicated by a large colored square.

The "What Can YOU Do?" sidebars provide ideas for children and teens that help them see how they can apply the spiritual truths in the healing story to their lives.

Bible verse sidebars provide a Bible verse with spiritual truths that Jesus would have known—also comments about the practicality of these truths to heal today.

Introduction

Jesus and His Healing Mission

Christ Jesus' healings inspired the people of Palestine in the first century A.D., and they inspire us today. While Jesus' background was humble, his words and works were mighty.

Jesus grew to manhood knowing that his mission was God-directed. Luke reports that at the age of 30, Jesus began his ministry. It was in the synagogue in Nazareth, where he had grown up, that he announced to those who had known him as a child and now as a man, that he had a mission—one that the prophet Isaiah had told them about many years before. He stood to read it,

> The Spirit of the Lord is upon me, because he hath anointed me to preach the gospel to the poor; he hath sent me to heal the brokenhearted, to preach deliverance to the captives, and recovering of sight to the blind, to set at liberty them that are bruised, to preach the acceptable year of the Lord (Luke 4:18, 19).

All eyes were on this gentle, loving man as he told the people that this Scripture was fulfilled that day. They were in the presence of the man who was bringing good news to the world. This message of God's infinite power and love for His children would heal sickness and sin and restore life.

For the next three years, Jesus took this message into the cities and regions of Palestine. Matthew tells us: "And there followed him great multitudes of people from Galilee, and from Decapolis, and from Jerusalem, and from Judæa, and from beyond Jordan" (Matthew 4:25). Although most of Jesus' works occurred in Galilee, he also healed in other regions, such as Samaria and Phoenicia in Syria. "Beyond Jordan" refers to the regions to the east of the Jordan River that included Decapolis, Perea, and Gaulanitis.

He taught, he preached, he healed the sick and sinning, and he brought people back to life. The Bible records 30 individual healings. But it also tells us that Jesus healed many others. Here, Matthew tells of Jesus healing large numbers of people,

> And great multitudes came unto him, having with them those that were lame, blind, dumb, maimed, and many others, and cast them down at Jesus' feet; and he healed them: insomuch that the multitude wondered, when they saw the dumb to speak, the maimed to be whole, the lame to walk, and the blind to see: and they glorified the God of Israel (Matthew 15:30, 31).

Jesus sent out his closest disciples (as well as 70 others) to heal as he did. He told them,

> And as ye go, preach, saying, The kingdom of heaven is at hand. Heal the sick, cleanse the lepers, raise the dead, cast out devils: freely ye have received, freely give (Matthew 10:8).

And Jesus didn't leave his instruction to heal only with his disciples. It's clear that he expected all of his followers down through the ages to heal through spiritual means. He said,

> Verily, verily, I say unto you, He that believeth on me, the works that I do shall he do also; and greater works than these shall he do (John 14:12).

Introduction

Jesus' Times and the Dawn of the Messiah

Jesus was a Jew. His background was grounded in the Jewish belief in one God. He lived in a time when the Jews had very little control over their own lives. Many years before Jesus' time, Palestine was conquered by the Greeks. During that period, the Greeks tried to destroy the Jewish religion. Life for the Jews was extremely harsh. In 63 B.C. the Romans took over Palestine, and the Jews felt the enormous weight of that rule.

The major religious leaders of their times, referred to in the Bible as the scribes and Pharisees, developed a system of worship that was centered on everyday human observance of religious laws. Some of these laws were written; others were spoken. The intent of these laws was to help the Jews keep their faith centered in their belief in God. The effect, however, was that the laws were so restrictive and the details so minute that too often people focused on the laws more than on the inspiration and power of God.

This was the political and religious environment in which Jesus began his healing ministry.

Hundreds of years before Jesus' time and during periods of occupation of their lands by other countries, the Jewish people began to develop the idea that a Messiah would come some day to free them from their enemies. Many thought of this Messiah as a king from the family of David (see **Messiah/Christ** on page 5). Many thought of him as a priest. Others spoke of a prophet who would come. Old Testament prophets told of a coming Messiah and what could be expected when he came. In fact, when Jesus read from the prophet Isaiah one Sabbath day in the Nazareth synagogue, the passage was one that the Jews would have recognized as referring to such a Messiah.

But Jesus' idea of a Messiah was a new one. He brought people fresh insights about his mission. He brought them an understanding of the Messiah as a spiritual idea that would heal. This spiritual idea was his and everyone's relationship to God as God's spiritual, perfect children. If one had complete faith in this view of man created in God's image and likeness—whole, healthy, and free—and understood the all-power of God, then they would feel and experience the kingdom of heaven, or harmony. Healing would be the outcome. And Jesus proved this with wonderful, powerful healings. Multitudes of people came to Jesus to be healed. Seeing and experiencing healing, they began to realize that he must be the Messiah they had longed for.

Each step of the way in his ministry, Jesus worked to help the religious leaders and the people understand the concept of the Messiah he was presenting. But Jesus encountered much opposition. He was a threat to the scribes' and Pharisees' system of religion. As they saw it, they were in danger of losing their Jewish following if the people accepted Jesus' teachings.

The scribes and Pharisees were focused on their materialistic system of worship and their need to preserve this system. They refused to recognize Jesus' works as evidence of the Spirit or power of God—the basis of his system of healing. This prevented most of them from seeing the spiritual import of Jesus' teachings and healings. This was an import that blessed the world then and continues to bless as spiritual healing finds its rightful place in the 21st century.

Introduction

The Messiah/Christ concept is central to an understanding of Jesus and his healings. Many of the healing stories that follow will refer to this information about the Messiah/Christ.

Messiah/Christ: The Hebrew word for "Messiah" and the Greek word for "Christ" mean "anointed"— chosen and dedicated—to save or deliver. Many Jews believed the Messiah of the Old Testament was a special anointed king from the family of David, who would come someday. This king, the "Son of David," would get rid of all their enemies and set up a kingdom that would last forever. Other Jews believed the Messiah would be a priest who would purify the way Israel worshiped God. And others saw that a prophet like Moses would come. Isaiah told of a Messiah who would be a light not just for Jews but for the whole world. To the Jews, light was a symbol of God's purity and goodness, which would save people from all their troubles.

Before Jesus' birth, Mary was told by an angel that her son would be great and would be called the Son of the Highest and that God would give him the throne of David. It was said at Jesus' birth that a Saviour, Christ the Lord, was born. John the Baptist prophesied that a Messiah was to come, one who was "mightier" than he.

At the beginning of Jesus' ministry, when he read from Isaiah in the Nazareth synagogue, he declared that he was "anointed" by the Spirit to be the great prophet described in Isaiah, one who would bless all by helping the poor and captives and healing people. Later, when John the Baptist sent his disciples to Jesus to ask him if he was the Messiah, Jesus referred them to his "works"—"the blind see, the lame walk, the lepers are cleansed, the deaf hear, the dead are raised, to the poor the gospel is preached" (Luke 7:22).

Jesus didn't think of himself as an earthly king. He saw his role as fulfilling the scripture to heal and teach and to bring to light the "kingdom of God"—the reign of harmony. He saw the Christ as his—and everyone's—spiritual selfhood. He knew that God created man in His image and likeness and kept him that way. Therefore, man is always spiritual, whole, and complete. Jesus never allowed the material picture of sickness, sin, and death to have power or reality in his thought.

By knowing that the Christ, or his spiritual selfhood, was the only truth or reality, Jesus destroyed the "enemies" of sickness, sin, and death. And this understanding of the Christ brought the "kingdom of God"— complete harmony.

Jesus' life, teachings, and spiritual healings showed how clearly he understood his spiritual selfhood. People began to give him the title of "Christ," calling him "Christ Jesus." Christ Jesus is an example for us all. We, too, can heal as he commanded his followers to do, by understanding God's all-power and our spiritual relationship to Him.

In the recorded stories of Jesus' healings, names that refer to the Messiah are:

Christ
Holy One of God
Prophet
Son of David
Son of the Most High God
Light of the World
Son of God

Man Healed of Mental Illness (Capernaum)

Luke 4:31-37

*Another account of this story is found in **Mark 1:21-28**.*

Galilee: This was the region in the north of Palestine in which Jesus grew up and spent most of his healing ministry. Almost all the disciples came from Galilee.

Capernaum: This was a small city in Galilee where Jesus began his ministry. People with products of all kinds traveled through the city to the Mediterranean and Damascus. Roman soldiers were stationed there. Many people in Capernaum, including some of Jesus' disciples, earned their living as fishermen on the Sea of Galilee.

Sabbath/Synagogue: The Jews met in the synagogue to worship God on the Sabbath day, which is Saturday. Inside the synagogue were benches along the walls, a raised platform, oil lamps, and a cabinet to hold the Scriptures on scrolls. Men and women may have sat in separate places. "Chief seats" were reserved for elders and important visitors. Jesus once rebuked the scribes and Pharisees for taking these seats so that people could see them. The service consisted of prayer, singing psalms, reading from the Scriptures, and teaching. The man in charge, the "ruler," chose men to read and teach. Jesus was chosen to teach in synagogues many times. (See **Sabbath Laws** on page 29 and **Scribes, Pharisees** on page 25.)

Jesus left his hometown of Nazareth in **Galilee** and traveled to **Capernaum.** This busy city was on the shore of a beautiful lake called the Sea of Galilee.

While Jesus was in Capernaum, he taught in the **synagogue** on the **Sabbath** days. This is where the Jewish people met to pray and learn about God.

As the people listened to Jesus, they were amazed at his **word,** or teaching. Jesus was always listening to God's good thoughts. And when he taught the people, he spoke those thoughts that were from God.

Jesus was always praying—always knowing that God is good and is the only power. He was always knowing that God, Spirit, created everyone in His image and likeness. The people felt the power of the truths that Jesus told them. ■ They saw that Jesus' understanding of God's power and love healed people.

Word: In Greek, "word" is *logos.* One of the meanings of this Greek word is "something said, including the thought." In the Old Testament prophets are those chosen to speak God's word. To the Jews, God's word had power. When it was spoken, people expected to see an effect. In the New Testament, John speaks of the Word as being God. Therefore, the Word has all the force of the thought of God. When God's word is spoken, it is powerful. It heals and restores life. It was prophesied that Jesus was chosen to speak God's word. His teaching was based on the Scriptures. It was the "gospel" or "good news" about God's power and His love for all mankind. Jesus knew that God is Spirit and that He made everyone in His image and likeness. Therefore, everyone is spiritual and perfect—always loved and protected by God. Jesus understood that God is the only power or presence. He didn't allow anything but God's goodness and love into his thought. He didn't accept sickness or sin or death as having any power or any place to be. And this understanding healed the sick—instantly. People were amazed. They felt the power of his word—his teaching—even if they didn't understand everything he said. Jesus proved that the power of the word—or good, true thoughts—healed even when he wasn't present (pages 33 and 38). Mark tells us that Jesus' disciples showed that Jesus' teaching or "word" was powerful for them as well. They were able to heal, too (Mark 16:20).

Mark adds that Jesus "taught them as one that had authority, and not as the scribes" (Mark 1:22). (See **Scribes** on page 25.)

Laws of Cleanness: These were laws the Jews believed they needed to obey in order to be "clean" or pure in the sight of God. They believed that the sick, the sinning, the dead, Gentiles, certain animals such as swine, and people controlled by what they called unclean spirits were "unclean" or impure. They believed that if they touched or were touched by someone or something that was unclean, they became unclean, too. To be clean or pure again, the unclean had to take part in special purification rituals. (See **Gentiles** on page 39 and **Purification Rituals** on page 19.)

While Jesus was teaching on one of the Sabbath days, a man was in the synagogue who wasn't supposed to be there. This man was mentally ill. The people believed he was **"unclean,"** which means "impure," and they didn't want to be near him.

In those days, people believed there were invisible beings called **unclean devils** or **evil spirits** that could make their bodies and minds sick. The people in the synagogue believed a devil was in this man.

Suddenly, the man screamed, "Let us alone! What do you want with us, Jesus of Nazareth? I know what you're up to. You're the Holy One of God and you've come to destroy us!" The "Holy One of God" was another name for "**Messiah**." Many Jews believed the Messiah was an earthly king that God would send to help and heal them.

Jesus knew that what the people called devils were only bad or wild thoughts. He knew God, who is good and the one Spirit, is the only power and could destroy the wild thoughts.

Unclean Spirits, Evil Spirits, Demons, Unclean Devils, Devils: In Jesus' time people believed there were invisible beings that could get inside them, could speak for them, and could cause many kinds of diseases and disabilities. They believed these beings worked for the Devil or Satan (words that refer to that which is opposed to God).

Messiah/Christ: See page 5.

WHAT CAN YOU DO?

You may be somewhere when someone is out of control. It may even be scary to see this person acting that way. Like Jesus, you don't have to be afraid. God is always in control. That person is God's child. You can be still and calm in your thought and know that God takes care of that person— and takes care of you, too.

For God hath not given us the spirit of fear; but of power, and of love, and of a sound mind.

II Timothy 1:7

Jesus knew that the power of God, who is the one Spirit, was right there in that synagogue to heal the man. Devils were not real and, therefore, were nothing to Jesus. God, Spirit, is right here with us today, taking away fear and giving us calm, strong thoughts.

Imagine how scary this man must have been to the people who didn't know what Jesus knew. This man was out of control. No one knew what he would do next.

Jesus was not afraid. He stopped the man by shouting two strong orders: "Be quiet! Get out of him!"

Jesus knew that God is always in control. He knew that a devil, which is only a bad thought, had no power over God or this man.

Just then, the man fell down but was not hurt. Instead, he was quiet and calm. Jesus' strong command destroyed the fear of devils. All those wild thoughts were no part of the man. He was completely healed.

Everyone was amazed. They said to each other, "What a powerful word this is! Jesus gives a strong command to the devils, and they leave!" Jesus showed the people that the power of God—the one Spirit—destroys the fear of evil.

Because of this wonderful healing, the news about Jesus spread quickly around Galilee.

Peter's Mother-in-Law Healed of Fever

Luke 4:38, 39

*Other accounts of this story are found in **Matthew 8:14, 15** and in **Mark 1:29-31**.*

Sabbath/Synagogue:
See page 6.

Capernaum: See page 6.

Mark adds that there were others, including James and John, who left the synagogue with Jesus. It also states that the house they went to belonged to both Peter and Andrew. Andrew was Peter's brother and also one of Jesus' disciples (Mark 1:29).

Peter: This disciple is called by several different names: Simon, Peter, Simon Peter, and Cephas. Peter was a fisherman before he became Jesus' student. He was an eager student, quick and enthusiastic in anything he did. He often spoke for the other disciples. Peter became a leader in the early Christian church. The book of Acts tells of Peter healing a lame man and a paralyzed man and bringing a woman back to life.

Disciples: The Greek word for "disciple" means "learner," or "student." In the New Testament, this word often refers to Jesus' 12 disciples. But it could mean anyone—man, woman, or child—who is a student and follower of the ideas of a teacher.

Jesus was in the **synagogue** in **Capernaum** on the **Sabbath** day. He had just healed a man with a mental illness. He then left the synagogue ■ to go to the house of **Peter,** one of his twelve **disciples.**

He probably expected that a nice meal would be waiting for him at the house.

But when he arrived, someone in Peter's family needed to be healed.

It was his wife's mother who was sick with a fever. Her family must have been very worried about her because the minute Jesus arrived, they begged him to help her. Jesus was ready and willing to help. He knew that God is always present to heal.

Luke says this was a "great" fever, which indicates that it was a serious illness—possibly malaria (Luke 4:38).

WHAT CAN YOU DO?

You might be asked to pray for someone. What if you feel you're not able to pray because you think you're not big enough or that you don't know enough? It helps to remember that Jesus knew it was always God who did the healing. And anyone—big or little—can turn to God for healing.

Matthew says Jesus "touched her hand" (Matthew 8:15). Mark says Jesus "took her by the hand, and lifted her up" (Mark 1:31). (See **Laying on of Hands/Healing by Touch** on page 17.)

. . . be strong in the Lord, and in the power of his might.

Ephesians 6:10

Jesus stood up to fear and sickness with words that were strong and commanding. God makes us strong, too. Just like Jesus, we can say to any bad thought that would make us sick, "No! Get out! Spirit, God, has the only power. Only good has a place here." When we're sure of God's all-power, thoughts of sickness are destroyed—and we are healed.

Jesus went to the sick woman and stood by her. ■ He was always letting his thought be filled with good from God—always praying. He knew this woman was God's child and that sickness could have no power over her.

He gave a strong command to the fever that was like saying, "You have no power! You are nothing! Get out of here!"

And the fever was gone!

Immediately, the woman got up and began serving them a dinner. She didn't have to rest at all. She was strong and ready to work.

How happy she must have been to be able to serve everyone a nice big meal. It was a great way to say "thank you" for her healing!

Man Healed of Leprosy

Mark 1:40-45

*Other accounts of the story are found in **Matthew 8:1-4** and **Luke 5:12-15**.*

Galilee: See page 6.

Leprosy: In the Bible the word "leprosy" can mean a variety of skin diseases. If people had a skin disease, they had to go to one of the Jewish priests, who would tell them what kind of skin disease it was. If it was serious, the priest called it "leprosy." The priests were important religious leaders. They proudly took turns working at the Temple in Jerusalem. On certain occasions they said special prayers or blessings, blew large trumpets, and blew the shofar (a trumpet made from a ram's horn). They performed many rituals that the Jews believed would make people "clean" or pure. (See **Purification Rituals** on page 19.)

Laws of Cleanness: See page 8.

Laws of Cleanness—Leprosy: Those judged by a priest to have leprosy were called "lepers" and were said to be "unclean," meaning "impure." The priest told them to obey the laws regarding cleanness. Lepers had to live outside the town, away from anyone except other lepers. They were not allowed to go to the Temple in Jerusalem. The law said that if people touched or were touched by a leper, they would also become unclean or impure. Once a leper was healed, he had to go back to the priest to be declared "clean."

After healing Peter's mother-in-law, Jesus traveled all over **Galilee**. He taught and healed people who had many kinds of sicknesses, including **leprosy**. This was a kind of sickness that made a person's skin look ugly. The people who had leprosy were called "lepers."

Lepers had to obey certain **laws** of the Jews. They had to live outside the town. They also had to wear ragged clothes, cover the lower part of their faces, and call out "Unclean! Unclean!" to warn people not to get close to them or touch them. How sad and lonely lepers were.

One day a leper came to Jesus.

The man kneeled in front of Jesus and said so hopefully, "If you want to, you can make me clean. You can heal me."

Jesus didn't step back from this man like everyone else always did. He wasn't afraid of the man or his sickness or the Jewish law that said he couldn't touch him. Jesus didn't see this man as a leper. He knew God is Spirit and man is made in His image and likeness. Therefore, he saw everyone as spiritual and never having anything that isn't like God. He tenderly reached out and **touched** this man as he said, "Of course I want to help you."

This made the man feel so loved and cared for.

Laying on of Hands/Healing by Touch: In Bible times many people believed they could be healed when they were touched by Jesus or when they touched him or his clothing.

■ *Being touched by Jesus ("laying on of hands"):* The term, "laying on of hands," was a symbol for the power of God to heal. To Jesus, placing hands on someone didn't mean that the human hands had any real power in them to bless or to heal. Instead, it was an expression of love and compassion that helped remove the person's fear. In half of Jesus' 30 recorded healings, no mention of Jesus touching the person is made. In three of these cases, he healed people who were not even present with him. And in many of the healing stories, when Jesus touched people, the Bible records that he made it clear it was their faith that healed them.

■ *Touching Jesus or his clothing:* Many people believed that if they touched Jesus or his clothing they would be healed. Jesus was so spiritually minded that he was able to know people's need for healing. Those who reached out were healed because of Jesus' clear understanding of the all-power of God, who is Spirit, to heal.

Jesus' healings show that he was not afraid of sickness—no matter how ugly or painful it was. We don't have to be afraid of sickness either. The words of this psalm help us see that God is our health. Jesus showed this leper that God loved him and gave him good health. God gives us good health, too.

WHAT CAN YOU DO?

Do you know someone who is sad and lonely? Maybe this person is sick or in a wheelchair, and no one pays attention to him or her. A kind word, a smile, a hug can mean so much to others. And it blesses you, too. Jesus said, "Love thy neighbor as thyself." He loved even the people others wouldn't love—and you can, too!

Then, Jesus said, "Be clean"—knowing the man was already the pure, spiritual likeness of God. The minute he said this, the man was healed! His skin was smooth and beautiful. He was so happy!

Jesus showed that even ugly leprosy couldn't win out against God's power of good.

Then, speaking firmly to the man, Jesus said, "**Don't stop to tell anyone** about this healing. Go do what the **Jewish laws** say you should do, now that you are healed."

The man went on his way to obey the Jewish laws. But he was so happy to be healed that he just wouldn't be quiet about it. He told everybody he saw that Jesus had healed him.

Then, so many crowds began coming to Jesus that he couldn't go into the city. Instead, he had to stay in the country. Even there, people from all around found him and came to be healed.

"Don't tell anyone....": Jesus told some of the people he healed not to tell anyone about their healings. Here are some possible reasons why he said this:

☐ The people he healed were inspired and grateful. If they spoke out, the scribes and Pharisees might ask them questions they weren't ready for. Perhaps Jesus was protecting them. He didn't want them to lose their faith and inspiration.

☐ People might come to Jesus just to see something exciting happen. They might crowd out those who really wanted to learn about God.

☐ If crowds gathered around Jesus, the Jewish religious leaders might become jealous and try to get rid of him.

☐ Crowds might start calling Jesus "Messiah." Many of them were expecting an earthly king to save them. Jesus needed time to teach the people and show them by healing and raising the dead what the Messiah really was—the spiritual selfhood belonging to him and everyone. He wanted them to see that he expressed this Christ, and they could, too. (See **Messiah/Christ** on page 5.)

Purification Rituals: According to Jewish laws, people considered "unclean" or impure had to follow certain rituals to become "clean" or pure again. For instance, after lepers were healed, they couldn't return home until they did what the priests required. Lepers had to make offerings, shave their bodies, and wash themselves many times. The lepers' families and friends then believed they were healthy and clean, meaning "pure."

Man Healed of Paralysis

Mark 2:1-12

*Other accounts of the story are found in **Matthew 9:1-8** and **Luke 5:17-26**.*

Galilee: See page 6.

Leprosy: See page 16.

Capernaum: See page 6.

Luke adds that among the people who came to see Jesus were Pharisees and scribes from Galilee, Judea, and Jerusalem (Luke 5:17). These men had probably heard about Jesus' healings, the huge crowds that were following him, and the Sabbath laws and laws of cleanness that he had broken. They may have come because they were curious about his teaching or to see for themselves if he was breaking Jewish laws. (See **Scribes, Pharisees** on page 25, **Sabbath Laws** on page 29, and **Laws of Cleanness** on page 8.)

The Bible does not say whose house Jesus was in or how large it was. Perhaps it was the house of Peter, or Peter's mother-in-law, or another friend of Jesus. Some scholars think Jesus may have had his own house in Capernaum.

Word: See page 7.

Jesus was in **Galilee,** where he had healed many people, including a **leper.** As he traveled from town to town, he healed many other people. When he returned to the city of **Capernaum,** the news spread quickly that he was back.

Many people ▢ squeezed inside the house ▨ where he was staying so they could get near him. When there was no room for even one more person inside, the people crowded around outside the door.

Jesus taught them the **word** of God—that God is all powerful and always loves and cares for His children.

Just then, four men arrived who wanted very much to see Jesus. They were carrying a friend on a **bed** because he was **paralyzed**.

These men were bringing their friend to Jesus to be healed. But they couldn't get close to the door because so many people were there.

Did they give up and go back home?

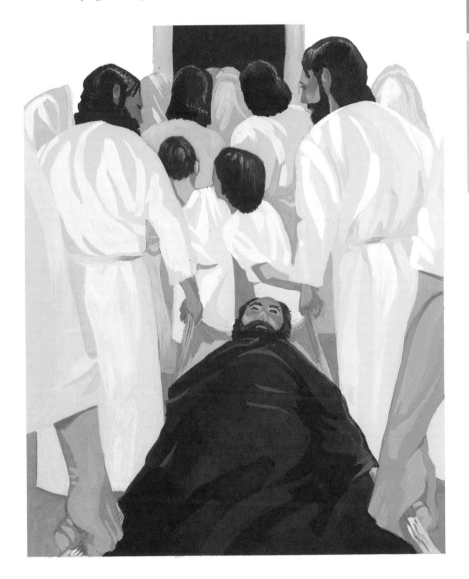

Beds: In Bible times beds were of various types. Some beds were simple floor mats, perhaps made of straw. Others had wooden frames and short legs and were often decorated beautifully. Some beds were like stretchers. They were made of fabric or woven straw with wooden poles attached, which made it easy to carry someone who was sick or disabled.

Paralyzed: The King James Version of the Bible says the man had "palsy." This word is used in the Bible to mean any disease that keeps a person from moving or having feeling in parts of the body.

Luke says the roof was made of clay tiles (Luke 5:19). However, in Galilee most roofs of the time were probably not made of tile but of branches, grasses, and mud placed over wooden beams.

WHAT CAN YOU DO?

Sometimes when you need help, it might seem impossible to get it. But you can always get help. When you ask God for an answer and then listen, an idea will come, just like it did for these four men. They found a very unusual way to help their friend! You're God's child, and He loves you so much that He is always showing you just what to do, also.

No! They didn't give up. These men must have loved their friend a lot! They were so sure Jesus could heal him that they found a way to get him to Jesus. They climbed up some outside stairs to the roof, carrying their friend on the bed.

Then they made a hole in the roof. This wasn't too hard to do because roofs were flat and often made of layers of branches, grasses, and mud placed over wooden beams. ▪

Imagine the people inside the house who were listening to Jesus. They could hear the men on the roof. Dirt and sticks were falling down on them. Wouldn't they have wondered what was going on?

Healing by Faith: In thirteen of Jesus' healings, "faith" or "believing" is mentioned as important in the healing process. The Greek word for "faith" means "conviction" or "belief." To have conviction means "to be firm." Jesus told his disciples to "have faith in God" and went on to tell them about the importance of not doubting (Mark 11:22, 23). When he asked people to have faith or to believe, Jesus wanted them to be firm in their understanding that he healed by the power of God. He said that everyone who believed could heal through this power. (Mark 16:17, 18).

Many people who were healed by Jesus had faith in him as the "Messiah" or "Christ." They sometimes called him the "Son of David" or "Son of God," which are terms that mean "Messiah" or "Christ" (see **Messiah/Christ,** page 5.) These terms came to stand for Jesus' spiritual nature—the influence of God, Spirit, in thought. This Christ-nature healed because it was the power of God. Jesus was constantly knowing that he was at one with God, that he was God's beloved Son. He knew God's power healed, and he proved it over and over again. He deserved to be called "Christ" Jesus because of his complete trust in God.

When people who were healed said they believed in Christ Jesus, they were saying that they understood Jesus healed through the power of God. By having faith in Christ Jesus and his teachings and healings, people were affirming the power of God in their own lives. This faith helped people see that they, too, could overcome sickness, sin, and death by following Christ Jesus' example.

When the hole in the roof was big enough, the men slowly lowered the bed, until their friend was lying right in front of Jesus! Jesus could see that these men had **faith** in God to heal their friend.

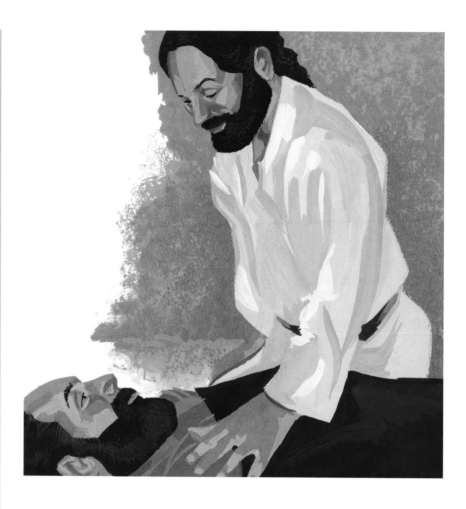

"Healed of your sins":
Several times in the Bible Jesus uses the words, "Your sins are forgiven." The term "forgiven" means wiped away, cast away, removed, healed.

In Bible times the Jews believed sin created a barrier or wall between sinners and God, keeping them from feeling God's love or help. They also believed sin caused people to be sick.

To be forgiven for their sins, people had to go through rituals required by Jewish laws. (See **Purification Rituals** on page 19.) But Jesus had a different idea about how people could be healed of their sins. When he said people's sins were healed or forgiven, he was seeing what was really true about them as God's children. He was helping them see themselves as completely good. This freed them to *do* good. And when their thinking and actions were healed, their bodies were healed, too.

Matthew tells us that Jesus also said to "be of good cheer" (Matthew 9:2).

Jesus spoke words of comfort and love to the man: "Son, you **are healed of your sins.**" ■ He knew the man needed to hear those words. In those days, people believed that those who were sick or paralyzed were being punished by God because they had sinned, meaning they had done bad things. This man was thinking of himself as a sinner.

But Jesus knew this man as God knew him—as God's perfect, spiritual child, who could never be bad or paralyzed. Jesus' words helped the man feel the power of God's love. These words healed him of the thought that he was a bad person. They freed his thought, and they also freed him so he could walk.

What a good thing for the man to hear that he was healed of his sins! It was good for everyone to hear.

Luke tells us that both scribes and Pharisees were present (Luke 5:21).

Scribes: These were men who copied the Jewish law (the "Torah"—the first five books of the Bible—which includes the Commandments) onto scrolls from other scrolls. They studied the Torah as well as many unwritten laws. Some scribes taught the meaning of all these laws and how people should obey them. But the scribes simply quoted words. Their teaching lacked the authority of Jesus' teaching. Jesus taught with absolute, unquestioned confidence in God's all-power. And this teaching resulted in healing.

Pharisees: The Pharisees were a group of men who loved to obey the Ten Commandments. But they also obeyed hundreds of other laws made by Jews through the years. Many Jews looked up to the Pharisees. So the Pharisees began to feel that they were more obedient to God's commands than other people were. And they felt they needed to watch everyone else to make sure *they* were obeying all the laws. The laws became so important to the Pharisees that they began to forget the real meaning, the spirit, of the Commandments, which was love for God and for others. Jesus, on the other hand, loved the true meaning of the Commandments. He taught people about God's love, and he proved this love by healing. If a Jewish law kept him from loving and healing, Jesus didn't obey it. This upset the Pharisees. It also bothered them that big crowds of people were following Jesus and not them.

But not everyone liked those words.

Some **scribes** and **Pharisees** were sitting there, listening to Jesus, and they didn't like those words.

Blasphemy: The Bible tells of a number of times that the scribes and Pharisees accused Jesus of blasphemy. In the Bible "blasphemy" means to dishonor God. The scribes and Pharisees said Jesus was breaking the Jewish law regarding blasphemy when he said he could forgive or heal sins. They said only God could forgive sins. Therefore, they thought Jesus was acting like God. They also accused Jesus of blasphemy when he called himself the "Son of God" and when he said, "I and my Father are one." A person could be stoned for blasphemy.

They heard Jesus' words of comfort and thought to themselves, "How dare Jesus talk that way! He's acting like God by healing the man's sins. **Only God can heal sins.**"

But Jesus knew what they were thinking. So he turned to the scribes and Pharisees and said, "Why are you thinking such things? Which is easier to say to this man who is paralyzed—'You are healed of your sins' or 'Get up, pick up your bed, and walk'?"

It would have been easier for Jesus if he had simply told the man to stand up, pick up his bed, and walk. Jesus wouldn't have gotten into trouble with the Pharisees. But, instead, he chose words of comfort that the man needed to hear.

Son of Man/Son of God:
Jesus called himself both the "Son of man" and the "Son of God." When he called himself the Son of man, he was referring to himself as a human being like any other person. When he called himself the Son of God, he was referring to his spiritual nature. Although Jesus knew that all people are children of God, he understood and demonstrated his sonship more perfectly than all others.

By using both of these terms for himself, perhaps Jesus wanted people to see that although he was human, it was his spirituality that enabled him to heal. This may have helped people understand that their own power to heal was a result of their spiritual nature as sons and daughters of God, with absolute faith in God's love and all-power. Jesus wanted them to know that they could heal as he did. Other names for Son of God are "Messiah" and "Christ." (See **Messiah/Christ** on page 5.)

Then Jesus told them, "I will show you that the **Son of man** does have power to heal people of sins." "Son of man" was a name Jesus often used for himself.

He then turned and looked at the man on the bed. They all watched to see what he would do.

Whosoever is born of God doth not commit sin; for his seed remaineth in him: and he cannot sin, because he is born of God.

I John 3:9

Jesus knew that God, who is Spirit, created His children in His image and likeness, without sin. This view of everyone as completely good and never punished by God, healed the sick. It's great to know that this truth is meant for us, too! Seeing ourselves as God sees us heals both sin and sickness.

Matthew adds that the crowd glorified, or praised, God because He "had given such power unto men" (Matthew 9:8).

Jesus said to the man, "Get up, pick up your bed, and go home." Instantly, the man did it! While they all watched, he stood up, picked up his bed, and walked out through the crowd.

When everyone saw the man walking, they knew that the man's sins must have been healed, just as Jesus had said.

The crowd was amazed. They all knew that it was God's power that healed the man. So they praised God, saying, "We've never seen anything like this! Thank you, God!" ▪

Man with Withered Hand Healed

Luke 6:6-10

*Other accounts of the story are found in **Matthew 12:9-13** and **Mark 3:1-5**.*

Galilee: See page 6.

Sabbath/Synagogue: See page 6.

Scribes, Pharisees: See page 25.

See "Man Healed of Mental Illness (Capernaum)," on page 6.

Sabbath Laws: "Sabbath" in Hebrew means "rest." Genesis says that God "rested on the seventh day." The Jews call this day the "Sabbath." This is the day God knew that His creation was complete, and He blessed this day (Genesis 2:2,3). The Fourth Commandment refers to this blessing: "Remember the Sabbath day, to keep it holy." The Jews believed that the way to keep the Sabbath holy was to do no work. Their laws listed many things that should not be done on the Sabbath, including healing. But Jesus understood God's "Sabbath rest" in a deeper way. He knew that everything God created is good, and He keeps it that way. So Jesus "rested" as God did—satisfied in God's complete and perfect, spiritual creation. That kind of rest is active and good. It heals—every day. Jesus never stopped healing—no matter what day it was. He knew that doing good is the very best way to keep the Sabbath holy.

Jesus continued healing and teaching in the cities and the countryside. Then, one **Sabbath** day he was in **Galilee** teaching in a **synagogue.** Several **scribes** and **Pharisees** were there, too. But, as usual, they weren't there just to pray and learn about God. They were there to see if they could catch Jesus doing something wrong.

Perhaps they were thinking, "When he healed the mentally ill man ■ on the Sabbath, he broke a **Sabbath law.** Maybe he will heal again on the Sabbath, and if he does, we can find a reason to get rid of him." They probably didn't want so many people paying attention to Jesus instead of to them.

One of the people in the synagogue was a man whose right hand was withered. Perhaps his hand was not formed in the right way or it was weak and lifeless.

WHAT CAN YOU DO?

The Pharisees tried to stop Jesus from doing good. Sometimes when you're doing something good for someone else—like helping someone who needs a friend—other kids might try to stop you. They might tease you and call you names. If this happens, you can remember that Jesus didn't let anyone stop him from doing good. Nothing can stop you either. When you help others and do what's right, you're doing God's work, and this makes you truly happy.

When the scribes and Pharisees noticed this man's hand, they began to watch the man and Jesus very closely.

Jesus knew what they were thinking. He said to the man with the withered hand, "Stand up and come forward." Perhaps Jesus wanted everyone to see what was going to happen.

The man obeyed Jesus and went forward.

Remember that the Pharisees were thinking mean things about Jesus and wanted to get rid of him. They also thought he shouldn't heal the man on the Sabbath. But Jesus knew that when he was healing, he was doing good work—God's work—and God certainly approved of that. Helping and healing were the best way to obey the Fourth Commandment, "Remember the Sabbath day to keep it holy."

Jesus surprised them by asking them a question, "Does the law command us to do good and help people on the Sabbath or to do evil and hurt people? To save life or to destroy it?"

Matthew adds that Jesus continued his argument with the scribes and Pharisees. Jesus made them think some more when he asked them if one of them had a sheep that fell into a hole on the Sabbath, wouldn't he lift it out? Jesus explained that a man is worth much more than a sheep. Therefore, Jewish laws *did* allow someone to help others on the Sabbath (Matthew 12:11, 12).

God is my strength and power: and he maketh my way perfect.

II Samuel 22:33

Jesus knew that God created everyone in His image—perfect and spiritual. He knew God gives everyone strength and power. Jesus saw this man as God created him and knew God would never allow him to be less than perfect. This view of the man healed him—instantly. When we see ourselves and others as God created us, we can be healed, too.

Mark adds that Jesus "looked round about on them with anger, being grieved for the hardness of their hearts" (Mark 3:5). Jesus saw how stubborn and unloving the scribes and Pharisees were. He might have thought, "How sad that they miss the happiness of helping others on this Sabbath day."

Jesus looked each scribe and Pharisee in the eye, one by one. ■ Maybe he was waiting for them to answer his question. But they had no answer.

So Jesus turned back to the man and said to him, "Stretch out your hand!"

Jesus knew that because God is Spirit, His creation is spiritual. He didn't believe that any part of a child of God could be deformed or weak. God made all his children perfect and strong.

Then, the man stretched out his hand. And, look—it was just as good as the other hand!

A perfect healing on the Sabbath day!

Nobleman's Son Healed of Illness

John 4:46-53

Once, after Jesus had been in **Judea** for a while, he returned to **Galilee.** There he visited the town of Cana, up in the hills.

At the same time, 20 miles away in the city of **Capernaum,** an important man had a very big problem.

This man was a nobleman who probably worked for the king. The nobleman had a son who was very sick, and he was worried about him. He needed to find help. He had heard how Jesus healed people and that he was in Cana. Because the man loved his son so much, he immediately went up the long road to Cana to find Jesus.

Judea: This is the region in the south of Palestine. Jerusalem, where many of Jesus' healings occurred, and Bethlehem, where he was born, are in Judea.

Galilee: See page 6.

Capernaum: See page 6.

33

When the man found Jesus, he begged him, "Please come down to Capernaum with me and heal my son! He is going to die if you don't come right away."

Jesus said to him, "Unless you people see amazing healings happen, you won't believe."

Perhaps Jesus was talking about people who came just to watch him. What Jesus really wanted was for people to come to learn more about God and His loving care for everyone.

The man went on begging Jesus, **"Sir,** please come down to Capernaum before my child dies!"

Did Jesus leave Cana to go with the man?

No, he didn't. Jesus wasn't afraid that the boy would die. He knew the truth that God was this boy's life and that God was keeping him safe. So Jesus said to the man: "Go on home now. Your son is alive and well."

And do you know what? This man, who had been begging Jesus to come with him, **believed** those **words** of truth that Jesus said—"Your son is alive and well."

The nobleman wasn't afraid any more. He knew that God was taking care of his son and that he would live. He didn't have to see his son healed and happy before he believed.

In fact, his thoughts were so peaceful about his son, he didn't even hurry home. He stopped to spend the night and didn't leave until the next day.

Healing by Faith: See page 23.

Word: See page 7.

WHAT CAN YOU DO?

Have you ever wanted to pray for someone who was sick or hurt, but far away? Well, you certainly can! Just like the nobleman, you can believe the truth that Jesus knew. Jesus knew that God made everyone spiritual and that God is always with everyone, keeping them perfect and healthy. When you believe this and hold on to it, this is a prayer that brings healing to others, wherever they are.

John says, "Yesterday at the seventh hour the fever left him" (John 4:52).

In Bible times, people started counting the hours of the day at dawn, and ended at sunset. Dawn was about 6:00 a.m. The first hour would have been 7:00 a.m.

The man's son was healed at the seventh hour, which was 1:00 p.m.

As the nobleman went down the long steep road to Capernaum, he saw some of his servants coming towards him.

They probably couldn't wait to tell him the news: "Your son is alive and well!" This is just what Jesus had said!

The nobleman asked them what time it was when the boy began to get better. "At one o'clock ▮ yesterday afternoon, the fever completely left him," they answered.

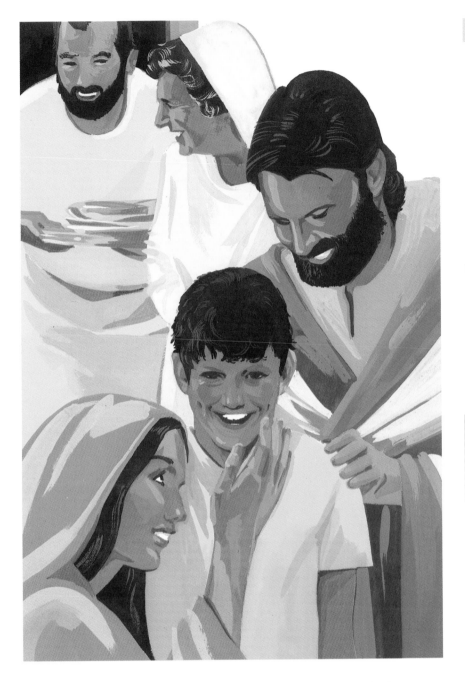

Jeremiah 23:23, 24

God, who is Spirit and Life, is everywhere. Jesus knew that God's power of good was always right with him. And he knew it was always with every one of God's children, no matter how far away they were, keeping them safe and healthy. That power of good is never far from any one of us but is always right at hand, helping us.

The term "believed" could mean that these people became Jesus' followers or supporters.

The nobleman then knew that his son was healed at the same time Jesus said, "Your son is alive and well." He, his whole family, and all the servants in his house "believed." ■ This means they trusted that Jesus healed through the power of God.

What a happy day!

Centurion's Servant Healed of Paralysis

Matthew 8:5-13

Another account of the story is found in Luke 7:1-10.

Galilee: See page 6.

Capernaum: See page 6.

Centurion: A centurion was a soldier in the Roman Army. The Romans ruled the country of Palestine (called Israel today). Their army was divided into legions, each with 100 centuries. A centurion commanded a century of about 50–100 soldiers.

Sir/Lord: See page 34.

Paralyzed: See page 21.

Luke adds that the servant, "who was dear unto him, was sick, and ready to die." Luke also tells us that the centurion sent some important Jews from the synagogue to ask Jesus to come and heal his servant. The men told Jesus that this centurion was a good man and loved the Jews so much that he had built them a synagogue (Luke 7:2-5).

Jesus had been teaching large crowds of people and healing in the countryside of **Galilee.** One day he came back to **Capernaum.**

The Romans ruled the whole country at that time, and many Roman soldiers lived in Capernaum. One of the soldiers, a **centurion**, came to Jesus begging for help. "**Lord**," said the centurion, "my servant is at home in bed, **paralyzed.** He is in great pain." ■

Jesus was always ready to heal anyone, any time, anywhere. He replied, "I will come and heal him."

The centurion then surprised Jesus.

Instead of leading Jesus to his home, the centurion said, "I'm not good enough for you to come inside my house."

Perhaps the centurion thought he wasn't important enough to have a great teacher and healer like Jesus come to his house. Maybe the centurion who was a **Gentile,** stopped Jesus from coming to his house because Jesus was a Jew. He knew about the Jewish law that said a Jew couldn't go into a Gentile's house. The centurion didn't want Jesus to do something wrong.

Since the centurion didn't think Jesus should come to his house to see his servant, how did he expect Jesus to heal him?

Gentiles: People who did not believe in the one God were called "Gentiles" by the Jews. Because Gentiles worshiped other gods, Jews considered them "unclean," or impure. So the Jews separated themselves from Gentiles to keep their religion pure. (See **Laws of Cleanness** on page 8.)

Word: See page 7.

WHAT CAN YOU DO?

Do you have faith that your prayer can heal someone who is sick? Jesus' prayers were powerful because he listened only to what is good. He said "No" to sickness. Just ordered it to stay out of his thought. You can be like Jesus and fill your thought so full of goodness and health, that there is just no room for anything else. God, who is Spirit, made everyone spiritual, whole, and healthy. How good it is to know this truth so completely and see that it heals others!

Here's how: The centurion understood that Jesus didn't have to be in the same room with the servant to heal him. He knew how powerful an order can be. He said to Jesus, "Just say the **word,** and my servant will be healed."

Then he added, "I'm used to taking orders from someone more powerful than I am. And I also know how to give orders. I tell one soldier 'Go,' and he goes. I tell another soldier 'Come,' and he comes. I tell my servant 'Do this,' and he does it."

The centurion knew that just as he had power over his soldiers, Jesus had power over sickness. The centurion got his power from the Roman emperor, while Jesus got his power from God.

Healing by Faith: See page 23.

Matthew says that Jesus continued to tell the Jews how important it is to have faith. The Jews believed that when the Messiah came, he would bring the kingdom of God. (See **Messiah/Christ** on page 5.) The kingdom would be ruled by the one all-powerful God.

Often, the kingdom of God was symbolized by a great and wonderful feast celebrating victory over enemies. Jews, who called themselves the "children of the kingdom," believed that they would sit down at this feast with the Messiah, along with Abraham, Isaac, and Jacob. Gentiles would never be included.

But Jesus told the Jews they couldn't join the feast just because they were Jews. It was their faith that would allow them to get in. In fact, Gentiles from many parts of the world, if they had faith like this centurion, would also sit down at that feast. And those Jews without faith would be cast out of the feast—the kingdom—into "outer darkness." They would be disappointed, bitter, and very angry (Matthew 8:11, 12).

Jesus may have been helping the Jews see that those without faith in the power of God to heal would miss out on the joy of the kingdom of God, His ever-present love and goodness.

Jesus was amazed at what the centurion said. He turned around and told the people following him, "This man's **faith** is very great. I haven't found a faith like this—even among the Jews." Jesus was saying that the centurion's trust in God's power to heal was much greater than the Jews' trust. ◼

When Jesus finished talking to the people, he turned back to the centurion. He said to him, "Go home now. What you've had faith in, has happened."

And at that very moment, his servant was healed.

Behold, I am with thee,
and will keep thee
in all places
whither thou goest.

Genesis 28:15

Jesus knew that this is God's promise to each of His children. Even if we seem to be all alone or far from help, God is with us, keeping us safe. No one is ever separated from God's love, care, and healing power.

Widow's Son Brought Back to Life

Luke 7:11-17

Capernaum: See page 6.

Disciples: See page 12.

Galilee: See page 6.

City Gate: In Bible times walls were built around cities for protection from enemies. People's homes were inside these walls. The walls were made of stone and were very thick. Usually, the only way to get in and out of the city was through the gate. This gate was made of wood and was thick and strong.

The day after Jesus healed the centurion's servant in **Capernaum,** he traveled with his **disciples** about 25 miles up into the hills of **Galilee** to the city of Nain. Many people followed him. They really wanted to hear what Jesus said and to see him heal people.

As they came close to the city, they saw a group of people coming out through the **city gate.**

The people were carrying the body of a young man on a bed. They were on their way to **bury** him.

In those days people showed their **sadness** about someone's death by crying loudly and playing flutes that made sad sounds.

The people were especially sorry for the young man's mother because she was a widow, a woman whose husband had died. This young man was the woman's only son.

When Jesus saw this mother in tears, he felt such **tender care for her.** He said to her lovingly and firmly, "Don't cry." He knew she didn't have to be sad. God *gives* life—He doesn't take it away.

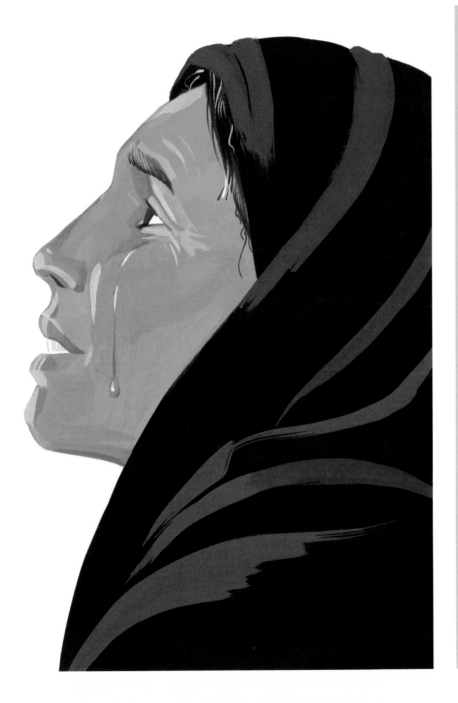

WHAT CAN YOU DO?
When you're crying because you're sad or hurt, it helps to stop crying and be quiet. Then you can hear God's messages and feel His love and comfort.

Jesus' Treatment of Women: In Bible times, people believed that women were less important than men. Many people thought of a daughter as just another mouth to feed. But a son could work for the family and carry on the father's name. Women were the property of their fathers or husbands. Yet they couldn't choose their husbands. Women had few opportunities to work. Therefore, a single woman might not be able to care for herself. She needed a man to help her— a father, brother, or son. Women were considered "unclean" for things that are natural to women, such as having babies. Most women were not educated. They couldn't read or teach in a synagogue. They weren't permitted to speak out in public. A man wasn't supposed to talk in public to a woman who was not related to him.

But Jesus was a reformer and introduced a new view of women. He treated them as equal to men. He spoke to them in the streets and synagogues. He taught women. He healed women. He included them in his parables. Women traveled with him and became his disciples. Two of his closest friends were Mary and Martha. Jesus helped women discover their individuality, freedom, and equality.

Laws of Cleanness: See page 8.

Laws of Cleanness—Death:
The Jews believed that the dead were "unclean" or impure. Jewish laws said that anyone who touched a dead body or bier (bed) on which a dead body lay was considered unclean, or impure. The laws also said that anyone who entered the house where a dead body was laid would be unclean. The unclean person was supposed to follow certain rituals to become clean, or pure, again. When Jesus touched this young man's bed, and when he entered Jairus' house and took Jairus' daughter by the hand, he was considered unclean. (See "Jairus' Daughter Brought Back to Life" in *Jesus' Healings,* Part 2.)

The Lord is my light and my salvation; whom shall I fear? the Lord is the strength of my life; of whom shall I be afraid?

Psalms 27:1

Jesus knew that the light of Life which is God shines everywhere, into every dark corner of sadness or fear. Nothing is more powerful than that light of Life. No darkness of death can put it out. How happy God's children are to know that God gives them life and keeps them safe forever. There is never anything to be afraid of.

Then Jesus went to the bed where the young man was lying and put his hand on it. The men carrying the bed were shocked—and stood still.

A **Jewish law** said it was wrong to touch the bed of a dead person. But Jesus didn't let a law like this keep him from bringing someone back to life. He knew that God, Life, is forever. He knew that death has no power over God's children because they are made in His image and likeness, spiritual and alive forever.

Jesus very calmly gave a strong command: "Young man, I tell you, get up!"

And the young man sat up. He began talking right away, and Jesus brought him to his mother.

The people were filled with wonder! They began to praise God, saying, "A great **prophet** has come to be with us again. ■ God is taking care of us."

After that, everywhere the people went, they talked about what an amazing thing they saw that day.

Prophets: Prophets are found throughout the Bible. They were people whose love for God was so strong and pure that they were always wide awake to God's word—the spiritual truths God was showing and telling them. Prophets blessed others by teaching them God's word. Moses, Elijah, and Elisha were prophets who showed the power of God's word by healing. Two of these prophets—Elijah and Elisha—also brought people back to life. As prophets, they saw God as all-powerful and loving. And this spiritual seeing resulted in wonderful healings. Anyone who sees and doesn't doubt God's power and love is a prophet and can heal, too.

Long before Jesus' time, Moses told of a great prophet who would come some day. Isaiah described such a prophet—one who was filled with the Spirit of God, who would preach good news to the poor, heal the broken-hearted, deliver the captive (in bondage to evil of any kind), give sight to the blind, and bring freedom to those who are weighed down with trouble. In fact, Jesus read these words in the Nazareth synagogue one Sabbath when he began his ministry and told the people that he was that prophet.

When Jesus brought this young man to life, the people may have realized that Jesus was the great prophet Moses said would come.

Woman Healed of Sin

Luke 7:36-50

Galilee: See page 6.

Pharisees: See page 25.

Jesus was in the **Galilee** area where he had brought a young man back to life. While he was there, a man named Simon, who was a **Pharisee,** invited him to dinner at his home.

Pharisees like Simon did their best to obey the Ten Commandments all the time, but they also followed hundreds of other Jewish laws. The Pharisees thought they needed these laws to help them obey the Commandments. But over the years, they began to pay more attention to the laws than to the Commandments. They also watched everyone else to make sure *they* were obeying all the laws.

Like the Pharisees, Jesus obeyed the Commandments. But unlike the Pharisees, he knew that what was most important about the Commandments was love—love for God and for others. So if a Jewish law kept people from loving and healing, Jesus didn't obey it.

Prophets: See page 47.

People had been calling Jesus a **prophet,** who is someone who listens to good thoughts from God and shares those thoughts with others. Simon probably agreed with this idea about what a prophet was. But as a Pharisee, Simon also thought a prophet should obey all the Jewish laws.

Simon may have invited Jesus to his house to find out if Jesus obeyed these laws. If he didn't obey them, it would prove to Simon that Jesus wasn't a prophet.

Dinner parties at people's homes were held either inside the house or outside in an open courtyard. Food was served on mats on the floor or on low tables. The people sat or lay on mats, cushions, or couches. Most people were welcome to come in to dinner parties, even if they weren't invited. They couldn't sit with the guests or eat the food, but they could sit against the walls, watch the guests eat, and listen to them talk.

During Simon's dinner party, a woman came in who was *not* welcome.

The woman is not named in this story. Traditionally, she has been called "Mary Magdalene," but she is not at all like Mary Magdalene in the Bible. The woman in this story was a sinner. There is no reason to think that Mary Magdalene was ever a sinner. The Bible says Jesus healed Mary Magdalene of seven devils. This probably refers to how serious her problem was rather than to sin (see Mark 16:1-10, Luke 8:1-3).

The King James version of the Bible calls this an "alabaster box of ointment" (Luke 7:37). In Greek this can mean either a jar of ointment or a bottle of perfumed oil.

People knew about this woman. They knew she was a sinner who had done many bad things. ▪

When she came in, the woman didn't sit against the wall and watch. She went right up to Jesus and stood by his feet. Big tears began to roll down her cheeks.

As this woman cried softly, she kneeled and washed Jesus' feet with her tears. The woman had no towel. So, with her long hair she very tenderly dried his feet and then kissed them. Next, she opened a small bottle of perfumed oil ▪ that she had brought. She gently poured this special oil on Jesus' feet.

As Simon watched Jesus and this woman, he thought to himself, "If Jesus really were a prophet, he would know this woman is a sinner. A prophet wouldn't let someone who has done bad things come close to him—and certainly he wouldn't let this woman touch him." Simon knew this was a **Jewish law** that Jesus was breaking.

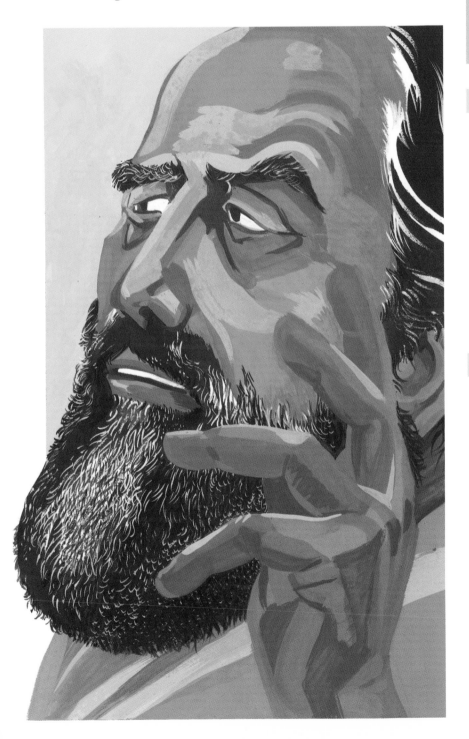

Laws of Cleanness: See page 8.

Laws of Cleanness—Sin: The Jews believed that sinners were "unclean" or impure and that anyone touched by a sinner would also be unclean or impure. A good Jew, and especially a prophet, was supposed to stay pure and holy.

WHAT CAN YOU DO?
If you meet people who look or act so different that others don't want to be with them, what can you do? You might think about what Jesus would do. Jesus always loved people and looked for goodness in them. You can do that, too. Loving others and seeing the good in them, brings healing and peace to them—and to you, too.

Teacher/Master: The Hebrew and Greek words that mean "teacher" or "master" were titles of respect. People called Jesus by these titles not because he had gone to a special school. It was because he spoke with great power and understanding when he taught about God and His laws.

Luke says that Jesus told a story to teach Simon a lesson. It was a story about two men who borrowed money from a banker. One borrowed 500 silver coins, and the other borrowed 50 silver coins. But they couldn't pay him back. The banker surprised them and told them that he forgave them both. That meant that they didn't have to pay him back because he erased what they owed. Then, Jesus asked Simon which one would love the banker more. Simon answered that he thought it would be the one who was forgiven more. Jesus told him that he was right (Luke 7:41-43).

✛✛✛

Here's one way to look at Jesus' story: The debtor who owed 500 coins was the woman. The other was Simon. The coins stand for how much each of them was looking for forgiveness (healing) for their sins. Jesus asked Simon, which one loved more. The woman's great love showed she had been healed of her many sins. Simon's very small amount of love showed he hadn't even seen any sin to be healed. Simon may not have realized that the man in the parable who loved less stood for him. But what Jesus said next may have helped him understand what he needed to learn (see page 53).

Jesus knew what Simon was thinking.

He said, "Simon, I have something to tell you."

"Of course, **Teacher,**" replied Simon. "Tell me." ■

Jesus' Treatment of Women:
See page 45.

It was the custom for Jews to welcome their guests and to show friendship and respect in various ways.

Jesus reminded Simon that he should have done the following for him as a guest in his house:

☐ Because it was a hot, dusty country much of the year, the host always provided water for guests to wash their feet. Sometimes a servant washed the guest's feet.

☐ The host greeted the guest with a kiss on the cheek, sometimes on both cheeks.

☐ The host poured a few drops of olive oil on the guest's head. (Oil was a symbol for gladness.) The host did this to honor his guest. To show even more respect, the host used perfumed oil, which was more expensive.

Jesus then turned to the woman and asked Simon, "Do you see this **woman**? When I came into your house, you didn't give me water for my feet. But this woman washed my feet with her tears and wiped them with her hair. You didn't kiss me, but this woman hasn't stopped kissing my feet. You didn't even put olive oil on my head, but this woman poured perfumed oil on my feet." ■

"Healed of your sins":
See page 24.

Then Jesus said to Simon, "I'm telling you that this woman has been **healed of her many sins**, for her love is very great."

Simon probably didn't understand what Jesus meant. Simon saw the woman as a sinner. Jesus saw her as God's child—as a prophet would see her.

Jesus knew that this woman had a deep love for the goodness and purity that he taught and lived. Her tears showed her sorrow for the bad things she had thought and done. Her kisses showed her meekness and willingness to understand Jesus' teachings. The oil she poured on Jesus' feet showed that she was grateful to be in the presence of this loving man. Jesus knew that her thought had changed and that she was healed of her sins.

But Simon had sinned and didn't even know it. He had not been kind to Jesus, who was a guest in his home. Also, he thought he was better than the woman. The woman had been healed of her sin. Her love showed she had been healed. Jesus pointed out that Simon's lack of love showed he needed to change his thinking and be healed of his sin.

Blasphemy: See page 26.

Healing by Faith: See page 23.

Peace: The word "peace" is used throughout the Bible. The Hebrew word for peace, *shalom*, has a rich variety of meanings including: prosperity, well-being, wholeness, health, security, harmony, happiness, quietness, calmness, rest, at one again.

Then, in front of the people at the dinner, Jesus said to the woman, "You are healed of your sins." Jesus knew the truth that God's children are always good and pure, the way God made them. This truth helped people feel their own goodness. Then, they were able to *do* what was good and right. Any bad thoughts, or sins, were wiped out—healed by the power of God's love and truth. Simon's guests didn't understand this. They said to themselves, "**Who does this man think he is, healing people of sins**?"

Jesus kept talking to the woman. He said, "It is your **faith** that has saved you." This woman trusted that the goodness Jesus saw in her was the truth about her, and this faith changed her completely.

She left the house that day with this loving message from Jesus, "Go in **peace**."

Thou shalt love the Lord thy God with all thy heart, and with all thy soul, and with all thy mind. This is the first and great commandment. And the second is like unto it, Thou shalt love thy neighbour as thyself.

Matthew 22:37-39

Jesus told his followers that all that was needed to obey the commandments was love—love for God and love for others. When we are loving God, we're letting nothing into our thinking but His love and its power. And when we are loving others, we're seeing them as God sees them—as His pure and perfect children. Jesus loved everyone. It didn't matter who the people were, where they came from, or what they had done. When Jesus loved this woman by seeing only the goodness of God in her, she was healed. We can heal as Jesus healed when we love as Jesus loved.

Man Healed of Blindness and Dumbness

Matthew 12:22, 23

Another account of this story is found in Luke 11:14.

Galilee: See page 6.

Jesus was in **Galilee**, where he was teaching and healing many people.

A man was brought to him who couldn't see and couldn't talk. ■ Almost everyone believed that a **devil,** or **evil spirit,** had made him this way.

But Jesus didn't believe this. He knew the truth that made people well. The truth is that devils, or evil spirits, are only bad thoughts or lies. It's a lie that a child of God can't see or talk. Jesus knew God is Love and tenderly cares for His children. His children are made in His likeness, spiritual, free, and perfect. This was the truth about this man.

Luke says the man couldn't talk, but he could see (Luke 11:14).

Unclean Spirits, Evil Spirits, Demons, Devils, Unclean Devils: See page 9.

Ye shall know the truth, and the truth shall make you free.

John 8:32

Jesus told his disciples that if they were good students, learned the truths he taught, and lived their lives using these truths, it would make them free. Jesus proved that the truth heals.
We can prove it, too. We can know the truth—that God, good, is the only presence and power and that He made us in His image and likeness. That means that since God, Spirit, is perfect, we are spiritual and perfect. So no matter what we may see with our eyes, the only thing true is what God gives us—perfection, goodness, joy, love, health. When we know the truth with all our heart and soul and do not doubt God's goodness and love—this heals. Just as the truth set people free from sickness, sin, and death in Jesus' time, the truth sets us and others free today.

So when this man was brought to Jesus, the truth Jesus knew healed him instantly. The man could see clearly and talk plainly. Imagine how happy this man was to be able to see and talk!

All the people there were so amazed at this wonderful healing. ◼

Here, the people asked, "Is not this the son of David?" (Matthew 12:23). "Son of David" was another name that people used for the "Messiah" or "Christ." (See **Messiah/Christ** on page 5.)

WHAT CAN YOU DO?

You may know someone with a problem that seems too hard to heal in an instant.

You can know that God who is good is infinite. That means God, good, is everywhere. Just think of it! There's no place for anything that is not good.

Jesus proved how powerful it is to know that God's goodness is infinite when he healed the blind and dumb man instantly. When Jesus saw something that wasn't good, he filled his thinking with the truth—that God, good, is everywhere. He never doubted this truth. Not for an instant. And the result was that people were healed— just as this man was. He could see and talk—right away.

You can know what Jesus knew. You can heal instantly, too. Each moment God is giving you good thoughts that help you see what is true and real. Those good thoughts are just as powerful to heal instantly in our time as they were 2,000 years ago. God's goodness fills all the space and all the moments, always and forever.

Bibliography

GENERAL

Deen, Edith. *All of The Women of The Bible*. San Francisco: Harper & Row, 1955.

Eddy, Mary Baker. *Prose Works Other than Science and Health with Key to the Scriptures*. Boston: The First Church of Christ, Scientist, 1953.

Eddy, Mary Baker. *Science and Health with Key to the Scriptures*. Boston: The First Church of Christ, Scientist, 1934.

Harris, Stephen L. *The New Testament, A Student's Introduction*. Mountain View: Mayfield, 1995.

Kee, Howard Clark., Young, Franklin W., Froehlich, Karlfried. *Understanding The New Testament*. Englewood Cliffs: Prentice-Hall, 1965.

Mann, Thomas W. *The Book of the Torah*. Atlanta: John Knox, 1988.

Robinson, Russell D. *Teaching the Scriptures*. Milwaukee: Bible Study, 1993.

Sergio, Lisa. *Jesus and Woman*. McLean: EPM, 1975.

Trench, Richard C. *Notes on the Miracles of Our Lord*. Grand Rapids: Baker, 1949.

Trueblood, Elton. *The Humor of Christ*. San Francisco: Harper & Row, 1964.

BIBLES

Amplified Bible. Grand Rapids: Zondervan, 1965.

Gaus, Andy. *The Unvarnished New Testament*. Grand Rapids: Phanes, 1991.

Good News Bible, The Bible in Today's English Version. Nashville: Thomas Nelson, 1976.

The Living Bible. Wheaton: Tyndale, 1976.

Hastings, Selina. *The Children's Illustrated Bible*. New York: DK, 1994.

The Holy Bible. Authorized King James Version. New York: Oxford University.

The Illustrated Family Bible. Edited by Claude-Bernard Costecalde. New York: DK, 1997.

New Jerusalem Bible. New York: Doubleday, 1990.

New Living Translation. Wheaton: Tyndale, 1996.

New International Version. Wheaton: Tyndale, 1984.

Peterson, Eugene H. *The Message*. Colorado Springs: Navpress, 1995.

Phillips, J.B. *The New Testament in Modern English*. New York: Macmillan, 1972.

DICTIONARIES AND CONCORDANCES

The Anchor Bible Dictionary. Edited by David Noel Freedman. New York: Doubleday, 1992.

Dictionary of Judaism in the Biblical Period. Edited by Jacob Neusner. Peabody: Hendrickson, 1966.

Dictionary of the Bible. Edited by James Hastings. New York: Charles Scribner's Sons, 1963.

HarperCollins Bible Dictionary. San Francisco: Harper. 1996.

Illustrated Dictionary of Bible Life and Times. Pleasantville: Reader's Digest, 1997.

International Standard Bible Encyclopedia Electronic Edition STEP Files. Parsons Technology, 1998.

The Interpreter's Dictionary of the Bible. Edited by George Arthur Buttrick. Nashville: Abingdon, 1962.

Quick Verse for Windows Version 5.0c. Cedar Rapids: Parsons Technology, 1992-1998.

Holman Bible Dictionary. Edited by Trent C. Butler.

International Standard Bible Encyclopedia. Edited by James Orr, 1998.

Strong, James. *The Exhaustive Concordance of The Bible.* Nashville: Abingdon, 1980.

Thayer, Joseph H. *Thayer's Greek-English Lexicon of the New Testament.* Grand Rapids: Baker, 1977.

COMMENTARIES

Barclay, William. *The Daily Study Bible.* Philadelphia: Westminster, 1975.

A Commentary on The Holy Bible. Edited by Rev. J.R. Dummelow. New York: Macmillan, 1939.

The Expositor's Bible Commentary. Edited by Frank E. Gaebelein. Grand Rapids: Zondervan, 1984.

Harper's Bible Commentary. Edited by James L. Mays. San Francisco: Harper & Row, 1988.

The Interpreter's Bible. Nashville: Abingdon, 1982.

The Interpreter's One-Volume Commentary on the Bible. Edited by Charles M. Laymon. Nashville: Abingdon, 1971.

JFB Commentary on The Whole Bible. Edited by Robert Jamieson, A.E. Fausset, David Brown. Grand Rapids: Zondervan, 1961.

Henry, Matthew. *Matthew Henry's Commentary on the Whole Bible.* New York: Fleming H. Revell.

The New Interpreter's Bible. Edited by Leander E. Keck. Nashville: Abingdon, 1995.

Stern, David S. *Jewish New Testament Commentary.* Clarksville, MD: Jewish New Testament Publications, Inc. 1995.

The Tyndale New Testament Commentaries. Edited by Canon Leon Morris. Grand Rapids: William B. Eerdmans, 1985.

The Wycliffe Bible Commentary. Edited by Everett G. Harrison. Nashville: Southwestern, 1962.

ATLASES

Atlas of the Bible Lands. Edited by Harry Thomas Frank. Maplewood, NJ: Hammond, 1990.

Oxford Bible Atlas. Edited by Herbert G. May. London: Oxford University, 1976.

DAILY LIFE IN BIBLE TIMES

Connolly, Peter. *Living in the Time of Jesus of Nazareth.* Israel: Steimatzky, 1983.

Derrett, J. Duncan M. *Jesus's Audience.* New York: Seabury, 1973.

Gower, Ralph. *The New Manners and Customs of Bible Times.* Chicago: Moody Press, 1987.

Great People of the Bible and How They Lived. Pleasantville: Reader's Digest, 1974.

Harper's Encyclopedia of Bible Life. Madeleine S. and J. Lane Miller. Edison: Castle, 1978.

Jesus and His Times. Edited by Kaari Ward. Pleasantville: Reader's Digest, 1987.

Thompson, J.A. *Handbook of Life in Bible Times.* Madison: Inter-Varsity, 1986.

Index to "What Can YOU Do?" Sidebars

Below are listed the "concerns" addressed in sidebars.

Index to Bible Verses

With this index, you will be able to find Bible verses in the stories and sidebars. In some cases, the Bible verses are paraphrased, rather than quoted or referenced. Bible books, chapters, and verses below are in the left column and in bold type. Page numbers are to the right of the verses.

General Index